CONTENTS

SESSION 1 Who Is He? 1
SESSION 2 Is He a Person? 11
SESSION 3 Is He Pentecostal? 23
SESSION 4 Is He Charismatic? 35
SESSION 5 Does He Baptize? 47
SESSION 6 Does He Speak in Tongues? 57
           Leader's Guide 67

THE GOD I NEVER KNEW

ROBERT MORRIS

STUDY GUIDE

The God I Never Knew Study Guide
Copyright © 2018 by Robert Morris

Content taken from sermons delivered in 2016 by Robert Morris at Gateway Church, Southlake, TX.

All Scripture quotations are taken from the New King James Version®. Copyright © 1982 by Thomas Nelson. Used by permission. All rights reserved.

All rights reserved. No portion of this publication may be reproduced, stored in a retrieval system, or transmitted in any form by any means—electronic, mechanical, photocopying, recording, or any other—without prior permission from the publisher. "Gateway Publishing" and "Gateway Press" are trademarks registered in the United States Patent and Trademark office by Gateway Church.

ISBN: 978-1-949399-81-3 Study Guide
ISBN: 978-1-951227-10-4 eBook
ISBN: 978-1-949399-41-7 DVD

We hope you hear from the Holy Spirit and receive God's richest blessings from this book by Gateway Press. Our purpose is to carry out the mission and vision of Gateway Church through print and digital resources to equip leaders, disciple believers, and advance God's kingdom. For more information on other resources from Gateway Publishing®, go to GatewayPublishing.com.

Gateway Press, an imprint of Gateway Publishing
700 Blessed Way
Southlake, Texas 76092
GatewayPublishing.com

23 24 25 — 9 8 7 6
Printed in the United States of America

1

WHO IS HE?

The Holy Spirit is the most misunderstood person in the Trinity. Knowing who He is and what His presence offers is vital to developing a powerful and fruitful relationship with God.

ENGAGE

Besides God, who is the most important or influential person in your life? Why?

WATCH

Watch "Who Is He?"
- Listen to how the Holy Spirit relates to us in the same way a person would.
- Watch for the benefits we receive through the Holy Spirit.

(If you are not able to watch this teaching on video, read the following. Otherwise, skip to the **Talk** section after viewing.)

READ

John 14-16 is a crucial passage for understanding the nature of the Holy Spirit and His function in the Trinity. These three chapters contain the last things Jesus said to His disciples before He went to the cross to be crucified.

Most theologians believe these chapters take place during the last 12 to 15 hours of Jesus' life. In chapter 14, Jesus speaks to His disciples at the Last Supper and makes it clear He is one with the Father. At the end of the chapter, in verse 31, He says, "Arise, let us go from here." Theologians believe Jesus enters the garden at the start of chapter 15, in which He teaches that He is the vine and His followers are the branches.

The main context of Jesus' message in His final hours is this: "I'm going away. Don't be troubled, though, because I am going to send someone else." He is introducing the disciples to the Holy Spirit.

> "And I will pray the Father, and He will give you another Helper, that He may abide with you forever—the Spirit of truth, whom the world cannot receive, because it neither sees Him nor knows Him; but you know Him, for He dwells with you and will be in you. I will not leave you orphans; I will come to you" (John 14:16-18).

Notice how Jesus says, "pray the Father," not "pray *to* the Father." This makes sense when you realize the word translated as "pray" is most often translated as "ask."

Jesus continually uses the words *He* and *Him* when referring to the Holy Spirit. The Bible never, ever, refers to the Holy Spirit as "It." Because He is not an "It." He is a person. If you don't see Him as a person, you won't develop a *personal* relationship with Him. The Holy Spirit is the third *person* of the Trinity.

In the Gospel of John, Jesus refers four times to the Holy Spirit as a Helper. In addition to the passage above, the Holy Spirit is described as a Helper in John 14:26, 15:26, and 16:7. In John 16:12–13, Jesus says He has many things to say to the disciples, but they cannot bear them yet. When the Holy Spirit comes, He will guide them into all truth. This answers any question as to whether the Holy Spirit speaks.

The word "Helper" comes from the Greek word *paracletos*. This is a compound word meaning "to come alongside." Jesus promises He will send someone to come alongside and help you.

Paracletos is also translated Consoler, Intercessor, and Advocate. The King James Bible translates it as Comforter. If you have a comforter on your bed, it may be designed just for looks. The Holy Spirit, however, is not for looks; He is for use.

The Holy Spirit is three things:

My Helper

The Holy Spirit helps me know what to say. You may have had a situation in the past in which someone asked you to pray, and a specific Scripture came to your mind. When you spoke the

Scripture out loud, the other person may have remarked, "I just read the same verse!" This was the work of the Holy Spirit.

The Holy Spirit also helps me know what *not* to say. When you hear yourself think, "I probably shouldn't say this," or "I probably shouldn't have said that," that is the Holy Spirit.

John 16:8-11 describes three ways the Holy Spirit helps us:

> "When He has come, He will convict the world of sin, and of righteousness, and of judgment: of sin, because they do not believe in Me; of righteousness, because I go to My Father and you see Me no more; of judgment, because the ruler of this world is judged."

Verse 8 says the Holy Spirit will convict us of sin, righteousness, and judgment. Why convict us of sin? If you don't believe you're a sinner, you won't believe you need a Savior. The apostle Paul writes, "No one can say Jesus is Lord except by the Holy Spirit" (1 Corinthians 12:3). It is the Holy Spirit's job to lead us to Jesus.

Second, the Holy Spirit convicts us of righteousness, meaning we are able to talk with the Father and have a relationship with Him. He convicts (or *convinces*) us that we now have "right standing" with God.

Finally, the Holy Spirit convicts us of judgment. When man first sinned, Satan became the ruler of the world. However, his power over your life ends the moment you enter into a relationship with Jesus. John 12:31 says, "Now the ruler of this world will be cast out." Satan no longer has any authority over you.

My Friend

The Holy Spirit is my friend, and He is not weird. You can be a normal person and believe in Him. It's the devil who has made people afraid of the Holy Spirit.

When the early Church received the Holy Spirit, thousands were saved in one day, and many others were healed and set free. At the turn of the 20th century, when the revelation and power of the Holy Spirit returned to the Church, Satan created controversy and put the emphasis on just one gift, causing confusion and fear.

The focus should not be on one gift (or "evidence") but rather on the benefits of the Holy Spirit. One benefit is the power to witness. Acts 1:8 says, "You shall receive power when the Holy Spirit has come upon you; and you shall be witnesses to Me."

Another benefit is love. 1 Corinthians 13 centers on love while chapters 12 and 14 concentrate on the gifts. Paul says that no matter how many gifts he has, without love, "it profits me nothing" (1 Corinthians 13:3).

A third benefit is the fruit of the Spirit (found in Galatians 5:22-23), and this fruit is experienced and expressed in a fourth benefit—the gifts of the Spirit.

My God

The Holy Spirit is my God. Some of us have been taught negatively about the Holy Spirit and somehow see His place in the Trinity as different than that of the Father and the Son. The Holy Spirit is a full and equal member of the Trinity. There are many verses in the Bible that mention all three members, including John 14:16, John 14:26, and John 15:26. At the baptism of Jesus in Luke 3:22, God the Father, God the Son, and God the Holy Spirit are all present.

The following passage proves the Holy Spirit is God:

> Peter said, "Ananias, why has Satan filled your heart to lie to the Holy Spirit and keep back *part* of the price of the land for yourself? While it remained, was it not your own? And after it was sold, was it not in your own control? Why have you conceived this thing in your heart? You have not lied to men but to God" (Acts 5:3-4).

When you lie to the Holy Spirit, you lie to God.

NOTES

_____

_____

_____

_____

_____

TALK

The following questions can be used for group discussion or personal reflection.

Question 1
The Greek word for the Holy Spirit (*paracletos*) is translated as Helper, Consoler, Intercessor, and Advocate. How do these terms aid your perspective on the nature of the Holy Spirit?

> IT IDENTIFIES THE NATURE OF THE HS FOR ME AND HIS ROLE IN MY LIFE

Question 2
Read John 14:25-26. What kinds of things do you think the Holy Spirit teaches you? How does He remind you of things?

> ALL THINGS — GODLY THINGS TO USE GOD'S WORD FOR MY LIFE TO MAKE RIGHT. A CLOSE RELATIONSHIP ALLOWS ME TO HEAR HIM AND ACT ON HIS MESSAGE

Question 3
Read John 16:12-13. What do these verses say to you about how the Holy Spirit communicates with us?

He will provide the Father's perspective on the things we are dealing with on life. He speaks to keep us on Gods Path

Question 4
John talks about the Holy Spirit convicting (or convincing) us of sin. Have you ever felt an inner conviction of sin stirred by the Holy Spirit?

Yes!

Question 5
How does Acts 5:3-4 prove the Holy Spirit is God?

It proves that to lie to Him - HS is the same as lying to God.

PRAY

If studying alone, ask the Holy Spirit to reveal the truth about Himself to you. If in a group, take some time to pray for each other as you think about the truths discussed in this session.

EXPLORE

Do you want to go deeper with this teaching? Here are some additional things to think about, pray for, or write about in your journal throughout the next week.

Key Thought

The Bible never, ever, refers to the Holy Spirit as "It." Because He is not an "It." He is a person. If you don't see Him as a person, you won't develop a personal relationship with Him.

Do you refer to the Holy Spirit as It or He? Do you feel differently when you think of Him as a person rather than a force or power?

He now.

Yes, seems more approachable

Key Verses
John 14:16-17; John 16:7-11; Acts 5:3-4

What truths stand out to you as you read these verses?

The HS is with us forever! I just need to rely on Him and not me. He is a gift from God - Jesus.

What is the Holy Spirit saying to you through these Scriptures?

Rely on me. Listen to me. Let me guide you.

Key Question
In this introductory session, we learned the Holy Spirit wants to have a *personal* relationship with us. Take a moment to think about some of the ways He has been your Helper, your Friend, and your God in the past week. In what ways could your relationship with God—and the Holy Spirit in particular—be more personal? What would this look like to you?

Key Prayer
Father, I am so grateful You sent Your Holy Spirit to be my Helper, Advocate, and Comforter. Help me understand the true nature of the Trinity and how important my relationship with the Holy Spirit is. Show me how to grow as Your disciple every day. In Jesus' name, Amen.

2

IS HE A PERSON?

The Holy Spirit has a distinct personality. As the third person of the Trinity, He has a soul. He has the mind of God, He knows the will of God, and He has God's emotions.

RECAP

In the previous session, we were introduced to the idea of the Holy Spirit as something more than a force or power. In fact, we saw how He is clearly an integral part of the Trinity along with God the Father and God the Son. As such, He relates to us as a person would. We learned it is important to have a personal relationship with Him. You cannot have a personal relationship with a force.

Describe any moments this week when you felt the presence of the Holy Spirit as a Helper, Friend, or God. How did you feel and respond differently than you might otherwise have if you had perceived the Holy Spirit as a force?

> ### ENGAGE
> What do you like to do for fun? If you had a free day to do anything you wanted, what would it be?
>
> ### WATCH
> Watch "Is He a Person?"
> - Look for the idea of the Holy Spirit as a person.
> - Watch for the facets of personality that comprise the Holy Spirit.
>
> (If you are not able to watch this teaching on video, read the following. Otherwise, skip to the **Talk** section after viewing.)

READ

As we learned in the first teaching, it is important to understand and perceive the Holy Spirit as a person. Remember, if you don't see Him as a person, you will never develop a personal relationship with Him.

Perhaps it is difficult to comprehend this idea because we say, "*the* Holy Spirit." However, "the Holy Spirit" isn't really His name. It's His description—His function. Each member of the Trinity has a function. God the Father functions as the Father, and God the Son functions as the Son. In the same way, God the Holy Spirit functions as the Spirit who indwells and empowers us and leads and guides us into all truth. His *name*, however, is God.

So, the Holy Spirit is a person, but what distinguishes a person? Is it life? A tree has life, but a tree is not a person. A simple definition is a person has a *personality*. Theologically speaking, a person has a soul. A person is not an inanimate object. The soul is made up of three parts: mind, will, and emotions. We think with our minds. We desire with our wills. And we feel with our emotions.

Is it possible the Holy Spirit is trying to help us think like God thinks, desire what God desires, and feel what God feels? According to Scripture, He lives inside you. The Holy Spirit can tell you what God thinks, desires, and feels about any situation because He is God.

The Holy Spirit Has a Mind

John 16:13 says, "When He, the Spirit of truth, has come, He will guide you into all truth." The Holy Spirit can guide you into all truth because He knows all truth. He is omniscient (*all-knowing*). The Holy Spirit knows everything.

God can never think of anything He's never thought of before. One of the benefits of being a Christian is you have someone living inside you who knows everything and has committed Himself to be your teacher. However, you will never ask Him for an answer if you don't believe He's a person. Why would you have a conversation with a force or a power?

The Holy Spirit Has a Will

Acts 16:6 says, "Now when they had gone through Phrygia and the region of Galatia, they were forbidden by the Holy Spirit to preach the word in Asia." To *forbid* means to exercise your will. Since the Holy Spirit has the will of God, and you'd like to know the will of God for your life, then why not get to know Him?

There are two ways you can know God's will: the general will of God and the specific will of God. We know the general will of God by His Word, and we know the specific will of God by His voice.

For example, if you want to know how to be married and how to treat your spouse, you should read the Bible. But if you want to know whom to marry, you won't find the answer in the text. The Bible will tell you how to operate your finances, be an employee, and raise children in a scriptural way. However, it will not tell you what job to take, where to live, or what house to buy. How can you know specifics for your life? The Holy Spirit. He will guide you into all truth.

If you want to know *how* to pray, it's in the Bible. Jesus taught us. But if you want to know *what* to pray, you have to know the Holy Spirit. None of us know what to pray on our own. Many people have heard Romans 8:28: "And we know that all things work together for good to those who love God, to those who are the called according to *His* purpose." But look at the two verses before it:

> Likewise the Spirit also helps in our weaknesses. For we do not know what we should pray for as we ought, but the Spirit Himself makes intercession for us with groanings which cannot be uttered. Now He who searches the hearts knows what the mind of the Spirit *is,* because He makes intercession for the saints according to *the will of* God (Romans 8:26-27).

We don't know what to pray without the Holy Spirit, and when we do know what to pray, it's only because He told us. To know the mind and will of God, we need to know the person living within us who has His mind and will.

There were times in history when only one person in an entire generation could hear God. There was even a time in the Bible when God did not speak to a single person for 400 years. In Acts 2, Peter says Pentecost is the fulfillment of God's promise made through the prophet Joel:

> "I will pour out of My Spirit on all flesh;
> Your sons and your daughters shall prophesy,
> Your young men shall see visions,
> Your old men shall dream dreams" (Acts 2:17).

This is the greatest time in history to be alive. God can speak to you personally. Every person can hear God through the Holy Spirit.

Jesus came to have a personal relationship with you. You can't have a personal relationship with someone through someone else.

Now, you should seek godly counsel. However, the question should be "Am I hearing God correctly?"—not "What is God saying?"

The Holy Spirit Has Emotions

All the fruits of the Spirit are characteristics of a *person*:

> But the fruit of the Spirit is love, joy, peace, longsuffering, kindness, goodness, faithfulness, gentleness, self-control. Against such there is no law (Galatians 5:22-23).

Ephesians 4:30 says, "Do not grieve the Holy Spirit of God, by whom you were sealed for the day of redemption." The Holy Spirit has feelings. In verses 25-29, we see lying, corrupt words, and stealing grieve the Holy Spirit. Verses 31-32 tell us to put away "bitterness, wrath, anger, clamor, and evil speaking." These also grieve the Holy Spirit.

Why does sin make the Holy Spirit sad? He loves you and knows sin will hurt you. Grief is a sadness you feel when you lose intimacy with a person. You grieve when a loved one dies because even though you will see him or her again in heaven someday, you lose intimacy with that person for right now. You also feel this kind of sadness when you see your children do something you know will hurt them. This grief is how the Holy Spirit feels when believers sin. As a believer, you don't lose your salvation when you sin, but you do lose your intimacy with the Holy Spirit, and this temporary separation grieves Him.

NOTES

_____
_____
_____
_____
_____
_____

TALK

The following questions can be used for group discussion or personal reflection.

Question 1
When you think of the Holy Spirit, what comes to your mind? Do you see Him as distant and mysterious or close and personal?

He is a Person whose Power lives in me. His Role is to Help and Comfort me

Question 2
Have you ever considered that God has a personality? What are some of His personality traits?

Loving, Kind, Slow to Anger, Gentle, Joy, Peace, Goodness and Faithfulness

Question 3
We know the general will of God from the Bible and the specific will of God by hearing His voice. In what ways does cultivating a relationship with the Holy Spirit help you know God's will? Can you think of any examples from your own life?

Getting Closer to God through Reading His Word Helps me get Closer to the H.S. AND God, I feel He Helps me more WHEN I DONT GRIEVE Him.

Question 4
Read Ephesians 5:25-32. According to this passage, what things grieve the Holy Spirit?

NOT CARING FOR MY WIFE PROPERLY, AND LOVING Her more than MYSELF.

Question 5
Why is it important not to grieve the Holy Spirit? Are there any issues in your life you need to confess and make right with Him?

Grieving The Holy Spirit Compromises MY Relationship WITH Him.

PRAY

If studying alone, ask the Holy Spirit to reveal the truth about Himself to you. If in a group, take some time to pray for each other as you think about the truths discussed in this session.

EXPLORE

Do you want to go deeper with this teaching? Here are some additional things to think about, pray for, or write about in your journal throughout the next week.

Key Thought

> You have someone living inside you who knows everything about everything and has committed Himself to be your teacher. But you'll never ask Him for the answer unless you believe He's a person.

How can we get to know the Holy Spirit better now that we know Him as a person with a mind, a will, and emotions?

It opens up a new perspective on what my relationship can be. I can talk to Him like a friend. I need to initiate this on my own by reaching out and asking Him.

Key Verses
John 16:13; Romans 8:26-28; Ephesians 4:25-32; Galatians 5:22-23

What truths stand out to you as you read these verses?

He wants to guide me and providing feedback from God. Do not grieve the Holy Spirit. Embrace and apply the fruits of the Spirit.

What is the Holy Spirit saying to you through these Scriptures?

Come close to me and exude the fruits of the Spirit

Key Question
Since the Holy Spirit is a person with a mind, a will, and emotions, what can you do to develop a more personal relationship with Him?

Key Prayer

Father, thank You for the person of the Holy Spirit. We want to know Him better. Teach us what is on Your mind. Guide us in Your general will and show us Your specific will. Help us never to grieve the Holy Spirit. In Jesus' name, Amen.

3

IS HE PENTECOSTAL?

In the Old Testament Pentecost was the celebration of God giving the Law to Moses on two stone tablets. In Acts 2 God gave the Holy Spirit to believers and wrote the law on people's hearts. You can still experience Pentecost today.

RECAP

In the previous session, we learned about the characteristics of the Holy Spirit as a person. He has a personality and a soul. With His mind, the Holy Spirit teaches us things we need to know in order to learn and grow as believers. With His will, He helps us discover the specific will of God. The Holy Spirit also has emotions, and He grieves when we separate ourselves from Him through sin.

Did you learn anything new since the last session that you think the Holy Spirit brought to your mind? Did the last session help you identify situations in which the Holy Spirit has shown you God's will for a circumstance or led you to an emotional victory?

> ### ENGAGE
> What is your favorite holiday? How does your family celebrate it?
>
> ### WATCH
> Watch "Is He Pentecostal?"
> - Look at the relationship between the Old Testament feasts and their counterparts in the New Testament.
> - Watch for ways we can experience Pentecost today.
>
> (If you are not able to watch this teaching on video, read the following. Otherwise, skip to the **Talk** section after viewing.)

READ

Is the Holy Spirit Pentecostal? If by "Pentecostal" you think of a denominational or historical definition, then no—the Holy Spirit is not Pentecostal. However, if you mean the biblical definition of the word *Pentecost,* that we believe fully in the person and work of the Holy Spirit, and that the event in Acts 2 is the fulfillment of the Feast of Pentecost, then yes—the Holy Spirit is indeed Pentecostal.

What Is Pentecost?

Pentecost was one of the three major feasts in the Jewish tradition, along with Passover and Tabernacles. The people of Israel gathered to celebrate these feasts in Jerusalem (and sometimes in other cities) during the first, third, and seventh months of the calendar year.

Passover, which occurred in the first month, represented when the spirit of death passed over the children of Israel when they were in Egypt. This celebration also included the Feasts of Unleavened Bread and Firstfruits. Pentecost was the second major feast and took place 50 days after Passover. The third celebration, the Feast of Tabernacles, occurred in the seventh month and also included the Feasts of Trumpets and the Day of Atonement. Together, these celebrations made up what we now know as the seven Feasts of Israel.

Pentecost celebrated the giving of the Law on Mount Sinai that took place 50 days after Passover. Pentecost simply means "50th." "When the Day of Pentecost had fully come" (Acts 2:1) refers to the 50th day after Passover. We have no reason to be scared of Pentecost. God knew His Son, Jesus, would be resurrected the day after the Sabbath and would be on the earth 40 days. The disciples would then pray for 10 days before the Holy Spirit came. Pentecost in Acts 2 occurred exactly 50 days after the resurrection. God even had this in mind when He gave the law in Leviticus 23:15-16:

> "You shall count for yourselves **from the day after the Sabbath**, from the day that you brought the sheaf of the wave offering: seven Sabbaths shall be completed. Count fifty days to the day after the seventh Sabbath; then you shall offer a new grain offering to the Lord" (emphasis added).

God gave the command to start counting on the day after the seventh Sabbath to match the 50 days between Jesus' resurrection and the outpouring of the Holy Spirit.

What Happened at Pentecost?

> There were dwelling in Jerusalem Jews, devout men, from every nation under heaven. And when this sound occurred, the multitude came together, and were confused, because everyone heard them speak in his own language (Acts 2:5-6).

This passage says people from every nation came together but were confused because they heard in their own language. Remember the story of the Tower of Babel in Genesis 11? Those people spoke one language, but because they came together in rebellion and pride, God used language to separate and confuse them. The people at Pentecost, on the other hand, gathered in humility. God restored to them a purer language, and they heard all about His wonderful works. Pentecost is the blessed reversal of the curse of Babel. Every nation, tribe, and tongue praising God was the fulfillment of the Feast of Pentecost, and this fulfillment continues today.

When the Law was given at Mount Sinai, there was a loud noise, fire, and a descending cloud. God wrote the Law on tablets of stone, but because of their disobedience, 3,000 people died that day. At Pentecost in Acts 2, there was also a loud noise, fire, and a descending cloud (the Holy Spirit). This time, however, God wrote His law on men's hearts, and 3,000 people were saved.

When God first gave the Law, the people of Israel couldn't keep it. When relying on our own strength, we can't keep it either. However, when the Holy Spirit comes, He writes God's righteous standard on our hearts. Jesus came to make us in right standing with God, and the Holy Spirit came to empower us to live righteously.

Can I Experience Pentecost?

> Then there appeared to them divided tongues, as of fire, and *one* sat upon each of them. And they were all filled with the Holy Spirit and began to speak with other tongues, as the Spirit gave them utterance (Acts 2:3-4).

Individual tongues of fire appeared on everyone in the Upper Room. No one was left out. "Tongues" is from the Greek word *glossa,* which means language. The tongue of fire on top of each person's head was a visible sign. Now, the people could not see the fire on their own heads; they had to believe by faith that they had fire just like everyone else. It is the same way today; we receive Jesus and the Holy Spirit by faith. There were 120 people in the Upper Room, and the gift of the Holy Spirit was for every one of them, not just the original disciples.

How can you experience this same empowerment?

> And being assembled together with *them,* He commanded them not to depart from Jerusalem, but to wait for the Promise of the Father, "which," *He said,* "you have heard from Me; for John truly baptized with water, but you shall be baptized with the Holy Spirit not many days from now" (Acts 1:4-5).

The disciples were told to wait for "the Promise," which is the gift of the Holy Spirit. In Acts 2 the Holy Spirit comes, and Peter answers the question "What do we do?":

> Then Peter said to them, "Repent, and let every one of you be baptized in the name of Jesus Christ for the remission of sins; and you shall receive the gift of the Holy Spirit. For the promise is to you and to your children, and to all who are afar off, as many as the Lord our God will call" (Acts 2:38-39).

"All who are afar off" includes every believer—this means you! God's promise is still available for you today.

Passover was fulfilled the day Jesus died. At the original Passover, the blood of a spotless lamb was shed for the sins of the people at 9 a.m. This was also the time of day when Jesus was nailed to the cross. At 3 p.m. the lamb was prepared to be placed in the oven, and at 3 p.m. they took Jesus' body off the cross and brought Him to the tomb. At Passover a father would hide the unleavened bread in the house, pull it out the morning after the Sabbath, and wave it before the Lord as a symbol of the firstfruits of the harvest. Jesus was pulled out of the tomb (resurrected) the morning after the Sabbath as the symbol of the firstfruits of the harvest to come.

Can you experience the fulfillment of the Feast of Passover and receive Jesus as the spotless Lamb who died for your sins, even though you weren't alive back then? Yes. Can you experience the fulfillment of the Feast of Tabernacles even if you are dead when the trumpet sounds? Yes. 1 Thessalonians 4:16 says, "For the Lord Himself will descend from heaven ... with the trumpet of God. And the dead in Christ will rise first." Because of the atonement of Jesus, we will be with God for all eternity.

In the same way, you can experience today the fulfillment of the Feast of Pentecost and be filled with the Holy Spirit just like those in the Upper Room.

NOTES

_____

_____

_____

_____

_____

TALK

The following questions can be used for group discussion or personal reflection.

Question 1
Did you grow up in a church environment that feared Pentecost, or were you taught a positive perspective?

_____

_____

_____

_____

Question 2
Why do you think the enemy works so hard to make people afraid of the Holy Spirit?

_____

_____

_____

_____

Question 3

What is the difference between the Old Testament Pentecost (when the Law was written down on stone) and the New Testament Pentecost (when the law was written on believers' hearts)? What does this look like today?

_____

_____

_____

_____

Question 4

Read Matthew 7:7-11. What does this passage say God will give to those who ask? Why was it important to Jesus to say this?

_____

_____

_____

_____

Question 5

Have you fully received the Holy Spirit?

_____

_____

_____

PRAY

If studying alone, ask the Holy Spirit to reveal the truth about Himself to you. If in a group, take some time to pray for each other as you think about the truths discussed in this session.

EXPLORE

Do you want to go deeper with this teaching? Here are some additional things to think about, pray for, or write about in your journal throughout the next week.

Key Thought
  Pentecost is the blessed reversal of the cursed judgment of Babel.

Read Acts 2:1-9. Imagine you were gathered with the believers during Pentecost. How would you have reacted if you had been present in the Upper Room?

_____

_____

_____

_____

_____

Key Verses
Acts 1:4-5; Acts 2:1-9; Leviticus 23:15-16; Acts 2:38-39

What truths stand out to you as you read these verses?

_____

_____

_____

_____

What is the Holy Spirit saying to you through these Scriptures?

_____

_____

_____

_____

Key Question
What have been your personal experiences regarding Pentecost and the baptism in the Holy Spirit? Have they been positive, negative, or nonexistent? How has your thinking changed now that you have learned more about Pentecost?

Key Prayer

Father, thank You for the gift of the Holy Spirit on the day of Pentecost. Thank You for writing Your law on our hearts. Please help us experience the fullness of the Holy Spirit in our lives every day. In Jesus' name, Amen.

4

IS HE CHARISMATIC?

Charismatic comes from the Greek word charisma, which means grace-gift. It is the instantaneous enablement of the Holy Spirit in the life of any believer to exercise a gift for the edification of others.

RECAP

In the previous session, we learned the Holy Spirit is Pentecostal, not in the sense of a denominational or historical definition, but as the fulfillment of the Feast of Pentecost. This was fulfilled when the Holy Spirit was poured out on believers in Acts 2. We can experience Pentecost today.

Did you understand or experience the Holy Spirit any differently this week?

> ## ENGAGE
> What is your favorite movie?
>
> ## WATCH
> Watch "Is He Charismatic?"
> - Look for the different types of gifts God gives us through the Holy Spirit.
> - Consider your personal gifts in light of this teaching.
>
> (If you are not able to watch this teaching on video, read the following. Otherwise, skip to the **Talk** section after viewing.)

READ

"Charismatic" comes from the Greek word *charisma*, which means grace-gift. *Charis* is Greek for grace, and *ma* is Greek for gift. Charisma is the instantaneous enablement of the Holy Spirit in the life of any believer to exercise a gift for the edification of others.

Some people are afraid of this word, even though we sometimes use it when referring to an individual who is gifted. However, there is no reason to be afraid. According to the Bible, if you have a gift God gave you by grace, you are charismatic.

In 1 Corinthians 12:1, the apostle Paul says he does not want believers to be ignorant of spiritual gifts. Many people today are ignorant about the Holy Spirit because they have not heard or been taught correctly. The word translated as "spiritual" in this verse is *pneumatikos*, which means powered by the breath or wind.

You can only move in these gifts if you allow the Holy Spirit to breathe in you.

In this passage, Paul is responding to a previous letter to the Church in Corinth. 1 Corinthians is actually the second letter he wrote, but we do not know what happened to the first letter. When he says, "now concerning," Paul is answering questions from the Corinthians. Like Paul, I don't want you to be uneducated about spiritual gifts.

There are four categories of gifts:

- Motivational (Romans 12)
- Manifestational (1 Corinthians 12)
- Ministry (1 Corinthians 14)
- Ministerial (Ephesians 4; These are gifts of Jesus)

We are dealing in this session with the nine *manifestational* spiritual gifts:

> But the manifestation of the Spirit is given to each one for the profit *of all:* for to one is given the word of wisdom through the Spirit, to another the word of knowledge through the same Spirit, to another faith by the same Spirit, to another gifts of healings by the same Spirit, to another the working of miracles, to another prophecy, to another discerning of spirits, to another *different* kinds of tongues, to another the interpretation of tongues. But one and the same Spirit works all these things, distributing to each one individually as He wills (1 Corinthians 12:7-11).

You don't "have" one of these gifts. They are given to each person as the Holy Spirit wills. Any believer can minister in any of the gifts as the Spirit empowers him to do so. The nine manifestational gifts are divided into three categories: the discerning gifts, the declarative gifts, and the dynamic gifts.

The Discerning Gifts

These include a word of knowledge, a word of wisdom, and discerning of spirits.

A *word of knowledge* means to know something *specific* without having learned it by natural means. Jesus moved in the gifts by the power of the Holy Spirit. For example, He knew the details of the woman at the well because He had a word of knowledge. When Jesus was on this earth, He laid down His divinity and ministered in the power of the Holy Spirit.

A *word of wisdom* is a divine answer or solution for a particular event. When Jesus healed the blind man in John 9, the people said they didn't know where this man Jesus came from. The healed man said He (Jesus) couldn't have done anything if He were not from God. The people could not give him a reply. God gave the healed man a word of wisdom—a wise answer.

Discerning of spirits means to be made aware of the presence of a demonic spirit. This gift was given when a girl was following Paul and others around, saying, "These men are the servants of the Most High God" (Acts 16:17). In spite of her words, this girl was possessed by a spirit of divination (she was a fortune teller), and

Paul didn't want a demon "helping" his ministry. He turned around and cast the demon out of her. How would you feel if the Holy Spirit showed you there was a demon coming against you, your marriage, or your business?

Discerning of spirits is not the same as general discernment. There is no gift of "discernment" in the Bible. Believers should be discerning, but most people who claim to have the gift of discernment are actually just very critical.

The Declarative Gifts

These include prophecy, tongues, and interpretation of tongues.

Prophecy is a message of encouragement from God through a person. It is meant to bring exhortation, edification, and comfort. Prophecy is *never* corrective. The spiritual New Testament gift of prophecy is always encouragement. Adding "thus saith the Lord" to the end of a word does not make it prophecy. Such a "word" is often simply criticism.

In 1 Corinthians 14:31, Paul says *all* can prophesy. Every one of you. It also says *all* may learn and be encouraged. (Notice it does not say "corrected.") We can all learn to hear God's voice and speak it in an encouraging way.

Tongues is a message from God in a language unknown to the person through whom the message comes. This is talking about the manifestation of tongues, not a prayer language. We don't routinely use tongues in our services at Gateway Church because it is a manifestation for believers, not for unbelievers. We have unbelievers and uninformed persons attending every weekend, and we don't want them to be confused.

Interpretation of tongues means understanding and expressing the thought or intent of the message spoken in tongues. Notice this gift is not called the "translation of tongues." Translation means word-for-word, but interpretation is the meaning behind the message.

In 1 Corinthians 14:5, Paul says he wishes all believers spoke with tongues. Tongues is an often-misunderstood but very important gift. The speaking of tongues along with their interpretation serves the same function as prophecy: encouragement.

The Dynamic Gifts

These include faith, gifts of healings, and working of miracles.

"Dynamic" comes from the Greek word *dunamis*, as used in Acts 1:8, meaning "power"—explosive power. The effects of these gifts can be explosive (like dynamite). When you witness, your words explode with power.

The gift of *faith* is a supernatural impartation of belief and confidence for a specific situation. It does not mean faith in general. The Holy Spirit may give you faith specifically when you are going through a difficult time.

Gifts of healings are supernatural endowments of divine health. Healing is a good thing. This doesn't mean you go around, and everyone you pray for gets healed. Instead, it means *you* get healed.

Working of miracles is divine intervention which alters our natural circumstances. Virtually all of us, at some time in our lives, have experienced what we would call a *miracle*. God has been doing miraculous things forever. Why would we ever believe He would stop? God will never stop doing miracles because God will always be God—and He is a miraculous God. It is the way He acts. He did them all through the Old Testament and New Testament. If you've been saved, you've experienced a miracle. It was a supernatural intervention in your life that altered your circumstances.

Don't be afraid of the manifestational gifts. Any believer can move in any of these gifts at any time when the Holy Spirit allows him to do so, and the result is always beneficial for everyone involved.

NOTES

_____

_____

_____

_____

_____

_____

TALK

The following questions can be used for group discussion or personal reflection.

Question 1

Can you think of a situation in which you could have used a word of wisdom?

_____
_____
_____
_____

Question 2

Read 1 Corinthians 14:1. Why do you think the Bible specifically tells us to desire spiritual gifts? Why do you think there is an added emphasis on prophecy?

_____
_____
_____
_____

Question 3

Read 1 Corinthians 14:31. Prophecy is meant to bring exhortation, edification, and comfort. In what ways would a prophetic word bring encouragement? Have you ever received an encouraging prophetic word?

_____

_____

_____

_____

Question 4

Have you ever received supernatural healing?

_____

_____

_____

_____

Question 5

Why do you think Satan would try so hard to discredit the gifts of the Spirit?

_____

_____

_____

PRAY

If studying alone, ask the Holy Spirit to reveal the truth about Himself to you. If in a group, take some time to pray for each other as you think about the truths discussed in this session.

EXPLORE

Do you want to go deeper with this teaching? Here are some additional things to think about, pray for, or write about in your journal throughout the next week.

Key Thought
> Jesus moved in the gifts by the power of the Holy Spirit.

Read 1 Corinthians 12:1. Why would God want us not to be ignorant concerning spiritual gifts? How would misunderstanding or lack of knowledge inhibit us from being used by God?

_____
_____
_____
_____
_____

Key Verses
1 Corinthians 12:1, 7-11; Luke 4:14; John 9:29-33;
1 Corinthians 14:5, 31

What truths stand out to you as you read these verses?

_____

_____

_____

_____

_____

What is the Holy Spirit saying to you through these Scriptures?

_____

_____

_____

_____

_____

Key Question
How can we posture ourselves so the Holy Spirit can give us these gifts to bless others? What does a willing heart look like?

Key Prayer

Heavenly Father, thank You for giving us such amazing gifts through the Holy Spirit. We want to be a blessing to others. Guide us as we learn to move in these gifts by allowing the Holy Spirit to breathe through us. In Jesus' name, Amen.

5

DOES HE BAPTIZE?

The Bible clearly shows three distinct baptisms. The Holy Spirit baptizes us in Jesus, the disciple baptizes us in water, and Jesus baptizes us in the Holy Spirit.

RECAP

In the previous session, we learned about the nine manifestational gifts of the Holy Spirit. There are discerning gifts, declarative gifts, and dynamic gifts. These are all still available for us today, and we should desire to receive whatever gifts the Holy Spirit distributes to us.

Do you feel more comfortable with the gifts of the Holy Spirit? Did you experience any this week?

> **ENGAGE**
> What brought you to your current church?
>
> **WATCH**
> Watch "Does He Baptize?"
> - Look for the three distinct forms of baptism.
> - Consider your personal experience with any of these baptisms.
>
> (If you are not able to watch this teaching on video, read the following. Otherwise, skip to the **Talk** section after viewing.)

READ

The New Testament teaches three distinct baptisms, and these baptisms have direct correlation to events in the Old Testament.

The Holy Spirit Baptizes Us in Jesus

When we get saved, the Holy Spirit baptizes us into the body of Christ. The Greek word for baptize is *baptizō,* which means to be fully immersed. In 1 Corinthians 12:13, Paul says we have all been baptized by one Spirit into one body.

The Disciple Baptizes Us in Water

The next step for a new believer is water baptism.

> "Go therefore and make disciples of all the nations, baptizing them in the name of the Father and of the Son and of the Holy Spirit" (Matthew 28:19).

Water baptism is a sign of this new life, but it is also more than a sign. It is a cutting of the flesh, a burying of the old person. When the Israelites went through the Red Sea, they were baptized. They left the old life of slavery behind and come forward into a new life of freedom.

Ephesians 4 says there is one baptism, but it also says there is one Lord. The Trinity (Father, Son, and Holy Spirit) is one God in three persons. Likewise, though there is one baptism, there are three distinct forms for the believer.

Jesus Baptizes Us in the Holy Spirit

> "I indeed baptize you with water unto repentance, but He who is coming after me is mightier than I, whose sandals I am not worthy to carry. He will baptize you with the Holy Spirit and fire" (Matthew 3:11).

In this verse John Baptist says the one coming after him—Jesus, the Messiah—will baptize us with the Holy Spirit. John could not have been speaking to the 12 disciples because they were not yet chosen. Instead, he was speaking to all believers.

Some people say the baptism into Jesus by the Holy Spirit and the baptism into the Holy Spirit by Jesus are the same. However, they can't be the same. Grammatically, they have different subjects. The baptism of the Holy Spirit is the baptism the Holy Spirit gives us when we are saved. The baptism *in* the Holy Spirit is the baptism Jesus gives us after we are saved.

Matthew, Mark, and Luke record only the third year of Jesus' ministry. John wrote much later and covered the first two years of Jesus' ministry. The birth, death, and resurrection of Jesus, the feeding of the 5,000, and the baptism in the Holy Spirit are the only accounts that appear in all four gospels.

> "I indeed baptized you with water, but He will baptize you with the Holy Spirit" (Mark 1:8).
>
> John answered, saying to all, "I indeed baptize you with water; but One mightier than I is coming, whose sandal strap I am not worthy to loose. He will baptize you with the Holy Spirit and fire" (Luke 3:16).
>
> "I did not know Him, but He who sent me to baptize with water said to me, 'Upon whom you see the Spirit descending, and remaining on Him, this is He who baptizes with the Holy Spirit'" (John 1:33).

Baptism involves three factors: salvation, water, and Spirit. Jesus is our example in these baptisms, as He is our example in everything. He was saved, He was water baptized, and He was Spirit baptized.

Salvation means we are born again. When we are born again, we are born as perfect children of God—not perfect in performance but perfect in our position because of Christ. We can't live a perfect life as Jesus did, but we are "in Christ" since we are baptized into Him. Jesus, of course, wasn't "born again" because He was born right the first time. He was born a child of God, already saved.

Jesus was water baptized as John describes, and He was also Spirit baptized. The Holy Spirit descended on Him immediately after His water baptism. If Jesus needed and received all three baptisms, how much more do we need them?

We see this pattern throughout the Bible. In Acts 2:38, Peter says to repent, be baptized, and receive the Holy Spirit. Five years later, in Acts 8:12-17, Phillip preaches in Samaria, and the people believe and are water baptized. In verse 14, Peter and John come to Samaria to see these new believers; they lay their hands on them and pray for them to receive the Holy Spirit. This takes place five years after Pentecost. The receipt of the Holy Spirit by the Gentiles in Acts 10 takes 10 years after Pentecost. Finally, in Acts 19:1-6, Paul finds disciples who had only been baptized into John's baptism. They had not heard of the Holy Spirit. Paul then baptizes them in the name of Jesus, and the Holy Spirit comes upon them. This occurs 25 years after Pentecost.

The apostle John writes:

> For there are three that bear witness in heaven: the Father, the Word, and the Holy Spirit; and these three are one. And there are three that bear witness on earth: the Spirit, the water, and the blood; and these three agree as one (1 John 5:7-8).

The three baptisms bear witness to the supernatural. When you get saved, you become a new person. When you get water baptized, the old person is cut off—left in the water, buried in baptism. And when you get Spirit baptized, you get power to walk in the new. God wants to give you this complete work.

Paul relates to this idea in 1 Corinthians 10. In verses 1-2, he reminds believers how the Israelites were baptized into Moses (their type of "deliverer"), the cloud (Spirit), and sea (water). In verse 11, Paul says the story of Israel's journey was recorded to serve as an example for future believers.

A final example is the Tabernacle of Moses. Moses received a vision of heaven, and God told him to draw on earth what he saw in heaven. To enter the presence of God in the Tabernacle, one had to pass through the outer courts to the Holy Place and then into the Most Holy Place. There were three items to pass on this walk:

1. The altar where the blood of the lamb was shed: Salvation.
2. The laver of water to wash with: Water baptism.
3. The flask of oil to anoint: Spirit baptism.

NOTES

_____

_____

_____

_____

_____

TALK

The following questions can be used for group discussion or personal reflection.

Question 1

The first baptism is repentance and belief (salvation). Take a moment and think about your salvation experience. What led you to repent and believe in Jesus?

_____

_____

_____

_____

Question 2

Were you water baptized after you were saved? Describe what this experience was like. What made it special?

_____

_____

_____

_____

Question 3
Read Matthew 3:11, Mark 1:8, Luke 3:16, and John 1:33. Why is it significant that the baptism in the Holy Spirit is mentioned all four gospels?

_____

Question 4
Read 1 John 5:7-8 and 1 Corinthians 10:1-2. How do these passages show the symbolism of all three baptisms?

_____

Question 5
Read Luke 11:11-13. What is the promise in this passage? Have you asked to receive the baptism in the Holy Spirit?

_____

PRAY

If studying alone, ask the Holy Spirit to reveal the truth about Himself to you. If in a group, take some time to pray for each other as you think about the truths discussed in this session.

EXPLORE

Do you want to go deeper with this teaching? Here are some additional things to think about, pray for, or write about in your journal throughout the next week.

Key Thought

When you get saved, you become a new person. When you get water baptized, the old person is cut off—left in the water, buried in baptism. And when you get Spirit baptized, you get power to walk in the new.

Read Acts 19:1-5. How does this passage show the importance of all three baptisms?

_____

_____

_____

_____

Key Verses
1 John 5:7-8; Acts 19:1-5; Luke 11:11-13

What truths stand out to you as you read these verses?

_____

_____

_____

_____

What is the Holy Spirit saying to you through these Scriptures?

_____

_____

_____

_____

Key Question
Have you received all three baptisms? If not, what do you plan to do next?

Key Prayer
Father, thank You for the three baptisms in Scripture. Thank You for the gift of salvation and water baptism. Thank You for baptizing us in the Holy Spirit so we can be empowered to live a victorious life. Allow the Holy Spirit to work through us with His grace-gifts. In Jesus' name, Amen.

6

DOES HE SPEAK IN TONGUES?

Speaking in tongues is biblical. There is the gift (manifestation) of tongues, which needs to be interpreted for edification. There is also a grace-gift of tongues, a prayer language that is not from God but to God. You can choose to pray in tongues.

RECAP

In the previous session, we learned about the three scriptural baptisms. These are salvation, water baptism, and Spirit baptism.

What did you learn about baptism that encouraged you? Did you commit to a baptism in water or the Holy Spirit that you did not previously have?

> ### ENGAGE
> Describe your perfect day.
>
> ### WATCH
> Watch "Does He Speak in Tongues?"
> - Look for the differences between the manifestation of tongues for interpretation and the grace-gift every believer can have.
> - Watch for ways that speaking in tongues can build believers up.
>
> (If you are not able to watch this teaching on video, read the following. Otherwise, skip to the **Talk** section after viewing.)

READ

The Bible clearly speaks of tongues in two ways. There is a gift of tongues (one of the manifestational gifts), which is a message from God that is to be interpreted to the church for edification. The Bible also teaches there is a grace-gift of tongues, which is a prayer language not from God but *to* God. Every believer can pray in tongues.

It's Scriptural

Paul describes the prayer language in 1 Corinthians 14:2:

> For he who speaks in a tongue does not speak to men but to God, for no one understands *him;* however, in the spirit he speaks mysteries.

When we pray in tongues, we are speaking to God in the spirit. Paul continues:

> For if I pray in a tongue, my spirit prays, but my understanding is unfruitful. What is *the conclusion* then? I will pray with the spirit, and I will also pray with the understanding. I will sing with the spirit, and I will also sing with the understanding. Otherwise, if you bless with the spirit, how will he who occupies the place of the uninformed say "Amen" at your giving of thanks, since he does not understand what you say? For you indeed give thanks well, but the other is not edified (1 Corinthians 14:14-17).

Paul shows the difference between praying in tongues (praying in the Spirit) and praying in your regular language (praying with the understanding). When you pray in tongues, your spirit prays, but your mind does not understand what you are saying. Paul says both ways of praying are beneficial, so he will pray with the spirit *and* with understanding.

Some people believe speaking in tongues is no longer available because they have been taught the Holy Spirit stopped operating when the Holy Bible was canonized in 393 AD. However, this is simply not true. The Holy Spirit is alive, moving, and speaking today. All of His fruits and all of His gifts are still available to us.

Paul obviously valued this prayer gift. In 1 Corinthians 14:18, he thanks God that he speaks in tongues more than all of his readers. He later concludes the chapter with this declaration in verse 39:

"Do not forbid to speak with tongues." Remarkably, some churches today still prohibit speaking with tongues, even though the practice is clearly scriptural.

It's a Benefit

> He who speaks in a tongue edifies himself, but he who prophesies edifies the church (1 Corinthians 14:4).

Some people use this verse as an attempt to put down praying in tongues. However, the conjunction "but" in this verse is mostly translated as "and." Paul is not putting down speaking in tongues. Rather, he is showing the difference between building oneself up privately (speaking in tongues) and building the church up publicly (prophesying).

Building oneself up is a good thing. There is nothing selfish about edifying your spirit. When in public, we should use language others can understand so they will be encouraged. In private, though, we do not have to understand the language for our spirits to be encouraged. Jude 20 speaks of building oneself up by praying in the Holy Spirit, and in Ephesians 6, the final piece of the armor of God is praying in the Spirit. We need all the building up we can get.

It's a Choice

You may say, "I don't have that gift." However, this prayer language is not the manifestational gift; it's a grace-gift available to all believers. In 1 Corinthians 14:14-15, Paul says,

> For **if** I pray in a tongue, my spirit prays, but my understanding is unfruitful. What is *the conclusion* then? I **will** pray with the spirit, and I **will** also pray with the understanding. I **will** sing with the spirit, and I **will** also sing with the understanding (emphasis added).

Praying in tongues is an act of your will. It is a decision you make that takes faith. If you have the gifts of teaching or giving, you can control them; you can choose how and when to use them. In the same way, praying in tongues is a choice. Why would Paul give instructions on how and when to use praying in tongues if it was uncontrollable? And since it is scriptural and builds you up, why would you *not* want to use it?

Not understanding what you are saying is not a reason to avoid praying in tongues. Jesus' teaching in Luke 11 shows that if the Father gives us a gift, it is for *our* benefit. If you are sincere, do you think God will give you a demon? Of course not!

You pray in tongues by faith. You open your mouth, get in the presence of God, and yield your tongue to the Holy Spirit. James 3:8 says, "No man can tame the tongue"—but the Holy Spirit can. If you have a problem saying the wrong thing—and you do, and so do I— why not yield your tongue to the Holy Spirit every morning?

NOTES

TALK

The following questions can be used for group discussion or personal reflection.

Question 1
What have you been taught in the past about speaking in tongues?

_____

_____

_____

_____

Question 2
Read 1 Corinthians 14:1-5. What is the difference between prophesying and speaking in tongues? Is Paul teaching believers shouldn't do either, or is he showing the appropriate usage for each?

_____

_____

_____

_____

Question 3

Read 1 Corinthians 14:14-15. Why does Paul pray "with the Spirit" and "with the understanding"? Are there benefits to both?

_____

_____

_____

_____

Question 4

Read 1 Corinthians 14:39. What stands out to you in this passage? How should this Scripture affect how believers and churches handle speaking in tongues?

_____

_____

_____

_____

Question 5

Read 1 Corinthians 14:5. Why do you think Paul wishes everyone spoke in tongues?

_____

_____

_____

PRAY

If studying alone, ask the Holy Spirit to reveal the truth about Himself to you. If in a group, take some time to pray for each other as you think about the truths discussed in this session.

EXPLORE

Do you want to go deeper with this teaching? Here are some additional things to think about, pray for, or write about in your journal throughout the next week.

Key Thought

If you have a problem saying the wrong thing—and you do, and so do I—why not yield your tongue to the Holy Spirit every morning?

Read Ephesians 6:14-18. How can you make wearing the armor of God and praying in the Spirit a regular part of your life?

_____

_____

_____

_____

_____

Key Verses

1 Corinthians 2, 4, 14-18; Jude 20; James 3:6-8

What truths stand out to you as you read these verses?

_____

_____

_____

_____

What is the Holy Spirit saying to you through these Scriptures?

_____

_____

_____

Key Question

Have you ever prayed in the Spirit? If so, how did it feel to use your prayer language for the first time? How did you grow more comfortable? If you have never prayed in the Spirit, will you choose to make use of this grace-gift?

Key Prayer

Heavenly Father, thank You for the benefit of praying in tongues. Thank You for giving us a way to speak directly to You and to be built up in the process. Please give us faith to yield our tongues to the Holy Spirit every day. In Jesus' name, Amen.

LEADER'S GUIDE

The God I Never Knew Leader's Guide is designed to help you lead your small group or class through *The God I Never Knew* curriculum. Use this guide along with the curriculum for a life-changing, interactive experience.

BEFORE YOU MEET

- Ask God to prepare the hearts and minds of the people in your group. Ask Him to show you how to encourage each person to integrate the principles all of you discover into your daily lives through group discussion and writing in your journals.
- Preview the video segment for the week.
- Plan how much time you'll give to each portion of your meeting (see the suggested schedule below). In case you're unable to get through all of the activities in the time you have planned, here is a list of the most important questions (from the **Talk** section) for each week.

SUGGESTED SMALL GROUP SCHEDULE

1. **Engage** and **Recap** (5 Minutes)
2. **Watch** or **Read** (20 Minutes)
3. **Talk** (25 Minutes)
4. **Pray** (10 minutes)

SESSION ONE

Q: Read John 14:25-26. What kinds of things do you think the Holy Spirit teaches you? How does He remind you of things?

Q: John talks about the Holy Spirit convicting (or convincing) us of sin. Have you ever felt an inner conviction of sin stirred by the Holy Spirit?

SESSION TWO

Q: When you think of the Holy Spirit, what comes to your mind? Do you see Him as distant and mysterious or close and personal?

Q: We know the general will of God from the Bible and the specific will of God by hearing His voice. In what ways does cultivating a relationship with the Holy Spirit help you know God's will? Can you think of any examples from your own life?

SESSION THREE

Q: Did you grow up in a church environment that feared Pentecost, or were you taught a positive perspective?

Q: What is the difference between the Old Testament Pentecost (when the Law was written down on stone) and the New Testament Pentecost (when the law was written on believers' hearts)? What does this look like today?

SESSION FOUR

Q: Read 1 Corinthians 14:1. Why do you think the Bible specifically tells us to desire spiritual gifts? Why do you think there is an added emphasis on prophecy?

Q: Why do you think Satan would try so hard to discredit the gifts of the Spirit?

SESSION FIVE

Q: The first baptism is repentance and belief (salvation). Take a moment and share your salvation experience. What led you to repent and believe in Jesus?

Q: Read Luke 11:11-13. What is the promise in this passage? Have you asked to receive the baptism in the Holy Spirit?

SESSION SIX

Q: What have you been taught in the past about speaking in tongues?

Q: Read 1 Corinthians 14:14-15. Why does Paul pray "with the Spirit" and "with the understanding"? Are there benefits to both?

Remember, the goal is not necessarily to get through all of the questions. The highest priority is for the group to learn and engage in a dynamic discussion.

HOW TO USE THE CURRICULUM

This study has a simple design.

The One Thing
This is a single statement under each session title that sums up the main point—the key idea—of the session.

Recap
Recap the previous week's session, inviting members to share about any opportunities they have encountered throughout the week that apply to what they learned (this doesn't apply to the first week).

Engage
Ask the icebreaker question to help get people talking and feeling comfortable with one another.

Watch
Watch the videos (recommended).

Read
If you're unable to watch the videos, read these sections.

Talk
Discuss the questions.

Pray
Pray together.

Explore
Encourage members to complete the written portion in their books before the next meeting.

KEY TIPS FOR THE LEADER

- Generate participation and discussion.
- Resist the urge to teach. The goal is for great conversation that leads to discovery.
- Ask open-ended questions—questions that can't be answered with "yes" or "no" (e.g., "What do you think about that?" rather than "Do you agree?")
- When a question arises, ask the group for their input first, instead of immediately answering it yourself.
- Be comfortable with silence. If you ask a question and no one responds, rephrase the question and wait for a response. Your primary role is to create an environment where people feel comfortable to be themselves and participate, not to provide the answers to all of their questions.
- Ask the group to pray for each other from week to week, especially about key issues that arise during your group time. This is how you begin to build authentic community and encourage spiritual growth within the group.

KEYS TO A DYNAMIC SMALL GROUP

Relationships
Meaningful, encouraging relationships are the foundation of a dynamic small group. Teaching, discussion, worship, and prayer are important elements of a group meeting, but the depth of each element is often dependent upon the depth of the relationships among members.

Availability
Building a sense of community within your group requires members to prioritize their relationships with one another. This means being available to listen, care for one another, and meet each other's needs.

Mutual Respect
Mutual respect is shown when members value each other's opinions (even when they disagree) and are careful never to put down or embarrass others in the group (including their spouses, who may or may not be present).

Openness
A healthy small group environment encourages sincerity and transparency. Members treat each other with grace in areas of weakness, allowing each other room to grow.

Confidentiality
To develop authenticity and a sense of safety within the group, each member must be able to trust that things discussed within the group will not be shared outside the group.

Shared Responsibility
Group members will share the responsibility of group meetings by using their God-given abilities to serve at each gathering. Some may greet, some may host, some may teach, etc. Ideally, each person should be available to care for others as needed.

Sensitivity
Dynamic small groups are born when the leader consistently seeks and is responsive to the guidance of the Holy Spirit, following His leading throughout the meeting as opposed to sticking to the "agenda." This guidance is especially important during the discussion and ministry time.

Fun!
Dynamic small groups take the time to have fun! Create an atmosphere for fun and be willing to laugh at yourself every now and then!

ABOUT THE AUTHOR

Robert Morris is the senior pastor of Gateway Church, a multi-campus church in the Dallas-Fort Worth Metroplex. Since it began in 2000, the church has grown to more than 100,000 active attendees. His television program airs in over 190 countries, and his radio program, *Worship & the Word* with Pastor Robert, airs in more than 1,800 radio markets across America. He serves as chancellor of The King's University and is the bestselling author of numerous books, including *The Blessed Life, Frequency, Beyond Blessed,* and *Take the Day Off.* Robert and his wife, Debbie, have been married 41 years and are blessed with one married daughter, two married sons, and nine grandchildren.

More resources for your small group by Pastor Robert Morris!

The Blessed Life **The God I Never Knew** **The End**

Blessed Families **Living in His Presence** **More Than Words**

Explore all available series at GatewayPublishing.com

The companion DVD is available to purchase separately at GatewayPublishing.com.